A CourseGuide for

The Mission of God's People

Christopher J. H. Wright

ZONDERVAN
ACADEMIC

ZONDERVAN ACADEMIC

A CourseGuide for The Mission of God's People

Copyright © 2019 by Zondervan

Requests for information should be addressed to:
Zondervan, *3900 Sparks Dr. SE, Grand Rapids, Michigan 49546*

ISBN 978-0-310-11100-9 (softcover)

Printed in the United States of America

CONTENTS

Introduction

Welcome to *A CourseGuide for The Mission of God's People*. These guides were created for formal and informal students alike who want to engage deeper in biblical, theological, or ministry studies. We hope this guide will provide an opportunity for you to grow not only in your understanding, but also in your faith.

How to Use this Guide

This guide is meant to be used in conjunction with the book *The Mission of God's People* and its corresponding videos, *The Mission of God's People Video Lectures*. After you have read each chapter in the book and watched the accompanying video lesson, the materials in this guide will help you review and assess what you have learned. Application-oriented questions are included as well.

Each CourseGuide has been individually designed to best equip you in your studies, but in general, you can expect the following components. Most CourseGuides begin every chapter with a "You Should Know" section, which highlights key terminology, people, and facts to remember. This section serves as a helpful summary for directing your studies. Reflection questions, typically two to three per chapter, prompt you to summarize key points you've learned. Discussion questions invite you to an even deeper level of engagement. Finally, most chapters will end with a short quiz to test your retention. You can find the answer key to each quiz at the bottom of the page following it.

For Further Study

CourseGuides accompany books and videos from some of the world's top biblical and theological scholars. They may be used independently, or in small groups or classrooms, offering quality instruction to equip students for academic and ministry pursuits. If you would like to engage in further study with Zondervan's CourseGuides, the full lineup may be viewed online. After completing your studies with *A CourseGuide for The Mission of God's People*, we recommend moving on to *A CourseGuide for Creation Care* and *A CourseGuide for Evangelism in a Skeptical World*.

CHAPTER 1

Who Are We and What Are We Here For?

You Should Know

- The mission of God's people flows from the uniqueness of the God of the Bible, supremely revealed to us in the uniqueness of Christ.

- Mission: all that God is doing in his great purpose for the whole of creation, which he calls us to cooperation with

- Missions: the multitude of activities that God's people can engage in to participate in God's mission

- "Sending" language in biblical stories can be seen in the stories and persons of Joseph, Moses, Elijah, and Jeremiah.

- Our mission flows from the prior mission of God.

- The goal of God's mission: the whole world

- Scope of our mission: the whole of creation

- Arena of our mission: everywhere

- The tension of the church's primary mission: proclamation and presence

Reflection Questions

1. In what way does all *our* mission flow from the prior mission of God?

2. Why should everything a Christian and a Christian church is, says, and does be missional in its conscious participation in the mission of God in God's world? How does it look practically to adopt this conscious posture?

3. Explain how we so easily fall into compartmentalized thinking when it comes to mission, splitting up our world into different zones. Instead, where does "missionary" work begin and end?

Discussion Question

1. What pops into your mind when you hear the word "mission"? What has been your experience with this word? Explain the difference between talking about *mission* (singular) and *missions* (plural), particularly using the analogies from science.

Quiz

1. When we think of "missions" we often think of cross-cultural missionary work and missionary societies, of evangelistic and church-planting missions, of long-term career missionaries or short-term missions, and of global networks of such agencies and individuals. What notion do all of these images have in common?

    a) Converting and evangelizing
    b) Sending and being sent
    c) Working and proclaiming
    d) All of the above

2. What sort of language is used in the following Bible stories: Joseph, Moses, Elijah, Jeremiah, and Jesus's disciples?

    a) Converting language
    b) Proclaiming language
    c) Sending language
    d) Missionary language

3. When we use the words "mission" and "missionaries," we tend to think mainly of what kind of activity?

- a) Social justice activity
- b) Biblical activity
- c) Conversion activity
- d) Evangelistic activity

4. To ask the question, "What is the mission of God's people?" is really to ask:

- a) "For what purpose do those who call themselves the people of God actually exist?"
- b) "What are we here on earth for?"
- c) "How are those who call themselves the people of God to go about evangelizing?
- d) Both A & B

5. Our mission flows from God's mission, and God's mission is for:

- a) The sake of his whole world
- b) The sake of the church
- c) The sake of the lost
- d) The sake of his elect

6. As soon as you think seriously about it, where is our mission field?

- a) In foreign countries
- b) On our own street
- c) At work
- d) Everywhere

7. When it comes to mission, the Bible is passionately concerned about:

- a) The kind of churches those who claim to be the people of God build
- b) The kind of actions those who claim to be the people of God do
- c) The kind of people they are who claim to be the people of God
- d) The kind of mission those who claim to be the people of God undergo

8. There is a range of questions we need to ask about "the whole church" that have to do with things like integrity, justice, unity and inclusion, and Christlikeness. What is the biblical word this describes that is as much a part of our missional identity as of our personal sanctification?

a) Justification
b) Holiness
c) Mission
d) Gospel

9. When it comes to the priorities of our mission, the questions raised create a tension between:

a) Proclamation and presence
b) Words and works
c) Sending and being sent
d) Both A & B
e) All of the above

10. The mission of God's people flows from the uniqueness of the God of the Bible, supremely revealed to us in the uniqueness of Christ, who is:

a) The source of our mission
b) The content of our mission
c) The goal of our mission
d) Both A & B
e) All of the above

ANSWER KEY
1. B, 2. C, 3. D, 4. D, 5. A, 6. D, 7. C, 8. B, 9. D, 10. D

CHAPTER 2

People Who Know the Story They Are Part Of

You Should Know

- Great Commission: the final words of Jesus to his disciples before his ascension, sending them out into the world to make disciples of all nations

- "I will also make you a light for the Gentiles, that my salvation may reach to the ends of the earth" (Is. 49:6b).

- The order of the major sections of the biblical story line (sequence, also conscious distractors): creation, fall, redemption, new creation

- Effects of the Fall: physical, intellectual, social, spiritual

- Sequence of Redemption History: call of Abraham; Exodus redemption; Sinai, Old Testament Israel, law, history, monarchy, exile and return, prophets, Psalms, wisdom covenant; incarnation of God in Christ; death and resurrection of Christ, new covenant; Pentecost, Holy Spirit, mission of the church; parousia, resurrection, judgment, new creation

- Prime Old Testament model for God's redemption began in the: Exodus from Egypt

- Results of Easter redemption: gift of the Holy Spirit and birth of the church

- Bible chapters spanning God's mission: Genesis 3 to Revelation 22

Reflection Questions

1. Why is it significant that the Bible does not begin the story at Genesis 3? Where does it begin instead, and what implication does this have for understanding the mission of God?

2. How have you seen or experienced the fall's effect on every dimension of human personhood and life on earth? Why and in what way is the mission of God good news for these realities?

3. How do the Holy Spirit and the existence of the church inform our theology of mission?

Discussion Question

1. It is helpful to visualize the biblical story as an actual line on which one can plot four major sections: Creation, Fall, Redemption in History, and New Creation. Briefly summarize and explain each of these sections.

Quiz

1. Where do a great number of books and sermons on the topic of Christian mission start?
    a) The Gospel
    b) The Great Commission
    c) The Ten Commandments
    d) The Exodus

2. It is helpful to visualize the biblical story as an actual line on which one can plot key points. What are the four major sections of the biblical story line?
    a) Creation, Fall, Redemption in History, and Heaven
    b) Creation, Fall, Salvation from Sins, and New Creation
    c) Creation, Fall, Redemption in History, and New Creation
    d) Evolution, Fall, Redemption in History, and New Creation

3. What fundamental plank of the Christian worldview and fundamental question of life does the creation narrative provide?

    a) Where did the universe come from and why does it exist and is it even real?

    b) What does it mean to be human?

    c) How did the world evolve?

    d) Both A & B

4. How has evil and sin woven their way into every aspect of God's creation and every dimension of human personhood and life on earth?

    a) Physically

    b) Intellectually

    c) Socially

    d) Spiritually

    e) All of the above

5. For whose blessing was the election of Abraham explicitly given?

    a) Israel

    b) The church

    c) All the nations of the earth

    d) Abraham's children

6. In Jesus, what entered into human history in a way not previously experienced before?

    a) The gospel of God

    b) The reign of God

    c) The law of God

    d) The help of God

7. What must be central to every dimension of the mission of God's people?

    a) The church

    b) The elect

    c) The law

    d) The cross

8. Just as the exodus redemption led to the creation of the covenant people of Old Testament Israel, what eschatological gift did the Easter redemption lead to?

   a) The Holy Spirit
   b) The church
   c) The law
   d) None of the above
   e) Both A & B

9. The Story of God — Creation, Fall, Redemption, and New Creation — can be viewed, from another angle as:

   a) The mission of God
   b) The gospel of God
   c) The movement of God
   d) The justice of God

10. God's mission is what Paul probably meant when he taught the Ephesian church about "the whole will [or counsel, or plan, or mission] of God" (Acts 20:27). It was a vast, comprehensive project of:

   a) Personal salvation
   b) Semitic salvation
   c) Cosmic salvation
   d) All of the above

CHAPTER 3

People Who Care for Creation

You Should Know

- Christians ought to be in the forefront of caring for creation. We have far more profound reasons for doing so, drawn from our faith and worldview, than merely prudential or self-serving ones.

- The Bible's beginning and ending: creation

- *Kabas*: subdue

- *Radah*: rule over

- *Abad*: serve

- *Samar*: keep safe

- False sequence of how a dualistic gospel works: individual, church, world, heaven

- True sequence of how Paul's gospel works: creation, church, world, individual

- Dimension of our ecological activity: creational and redemptive

Reflection Questions

1. What is meant by the statement that "we were human beings before we became Christians, and we don't stop being human beings when we do become Christians"? Why is this important to our identity and mission?

2. "See, I will create new heavens and a new earth" (Is. 65:17) suggests it is something God is already active in doing, not merely a future intention. Read Isaiah 65–66. What are the new heavens and new earth, and how will God later create these? How is he actively creating them now?

3. How is it that our ecological activity has both a creational and redemptive dimension?

Discussion Question

1. Human beings are people with a mission. We have a mission on earth because God had a purpose in putting us on it, which is encompassed in four Hebrew words. List those words, explaining and summarizing their meaning and how they describe our mission.

Quiz

1. The Bible begins and ends with:
   a) Creation
   b) The fall
   c) Redemption
   d) Heaven

2. The first mention of human beings in the Bible states two fundamental things about us, two things that are put so closely together that they are clearly connected:
   a) God made us in his image (both male and female); God intended us to use creation for our exclusive benefit
   b) God progressed our development into bipedal mammals (both male and female); God intended us to exercise dominion within creation
   c) God made us in his image (both male and female); God intended us to exercise dominion within creation
   d) God progressed our development into bipedal mammals

(both male and female); God intended us to use creation for our exclusive benefit

3. We humans have a mission on earth because God had a purpose in putting us on it, which is encompassed in four verbs. What are they?

   a) Subdue, dominate, serve, and protect
   b) Subdue, rule over, serve, and protect
   c) Use, dominate, serve, and protect
   d) Use, rule over, serve, and protect

4. The God-focused goal of human life (to glorify and enjoy God):

   a) Is exclusively human
   b) Sets us apart from the rest of creation
   c) Is something we share with the rest of creation
   d) Both A & B

5. Because we cannot articulate the *how* of creation's inarticulate praise, or indeed how God receives it:

   a) We should deny the fact that creation praises God
   b) We should not deny the fact that creation praises God
   c) We should be skeptical of the fact that creation praises God
   d) We should wonder whether it is a fact that creation praises God

6. Human life and creation are integrally bound together. How does the Old Testament emphasize this integral relationship between humans and the earth?

   a) Earth provides for us
   b) Earth suffers with and for us
   c) Earth is ours to use for our pleasure
   d) Both A & B

7. The Old Testament insists on a strong moral link between how humans behave on earth and the state of the earth itself. Specifically, what produces ecological stress?

   a) Human wickedness
   b) The fallenness of creation
   c) Global warming
   d) Satan's work in the world

8. According to Colossians 1:15–23, in Paul's mind, what is reconciled by the cross?

a) All humans and creation
b) Creation
c) Israel
d) The church

9. In what way does Paul link *Christ* and *creation* in the most comprehensive way?

a) Christ was there as the Son of God, even before creation existed
b) Christ is the source of the creation of the universe
c) Christ is beneficiary or heir of all creation
d) Christ sustains creation in existence
e) All of the above

10. What includes the whole of creation in the reconciling work of Christ, so that our mission is founded on the gospel and needs to reflect the length, breadth, and depth of the gospel?

a) The law
b) The Bible
c) The cross
d) The Holy Spirit

CHAPTER 4

People Who Are a Blessing to the Nations

You Should Know

- There is no blessing for us or others without faith and obedience.
- Genesis 12:1–3:

  "I will make you into a great nation,
      and I will bless you;
  I will make your name great,
      and you will be a blessing.
  I will bless those who bless you,
      and whoever curses you I will curse;
  and all peoples on earth
      will be blessed through you."

- The Abrahamic Commission: "Be a blessing"
- The Gospel: the good news that God intends to bless all nations, and to do so through Abraham and his descendants
- Sequence of covenantal blessing: blessing, salvation, obedience
- *Goyim*: all nations
- The ways Abraham is a model for our mission: leaving and going, believing and obeying

Reflection Questions

1. Paul said his calling as an apostle was "to bring about the obedience of faith for the sake of [Christ's] name among all the nations" (Rom.

1:5 ESV). In what way does this ambition carry with it strong echoes of Abraham?

2. The words *bless* and *blessing* shine through Genesis 12:1–3 like a golden thread, and they are set within relationships that are both vertical and horizontal. Explain how those relationships are blessed.

3. Explain what is meant by the statement: "All this talk of 'missional church' sounds to me like talking about a 'female woman.' If it's not missional, it's not church." Why can't church *not* be missional?

Discussion Question

1. How is the Abrahamic promise echoed throughout the Bible? Explain and summarize these echoes from the psalms and prophets, the Gospels, Paul's letters, and the book of Revelation.

Quiz

1. In short, what was God's promise to Abraham that through him all the nations on earth will be blessed?
   - a) The mission
   - b) The covenant
   - c) The gospel
   - d) The law

2. God's promise to Abraham only becomes clear when we see it against the darkening background of which chapters of the Bible?
   - a) Genesis 1–11
   - b) Genesis 12
   - c) Exodus 20
   - d) Deuteronomy 29

3. What kind of question does Genesis 1–11 pose; what kind of answer must God provide?
   - a) Salvation question, salvation answer
   - b) Creation question, creation answer

  c) Cosmic question, cosmic answer

  d) All of the above

4. What is the beginning of God's answer to the evil of human hearts, the strife of nations, and the groaning brokenness of his whole creation?

  a) The call of Abraham

  b) The call of Moses

  c) The call of David

  d) The call of the disciples

5. From the context of Genesis 12:1–3, the word "*blessing*" means:

  a) Fruitfulness and spreading

  b) Filling

  c) Abundance

  d) All of the above

6. If we see ourselves as those who have entered into the blessing of Abraham through faith in Christ, then the Abrahamic commission becomes ours. What is that commission?

  a) Be a blessing

  b) Share the gospel

  c) Save people

  d) Work for social justice

7. In Genesis 12, God addressed one man, Abraham, and promised to bring his blessing to humanity through one nation—his descendants. Who benefited from that choice?

  a) The one nation of Israel

  b) The elect of God

  c) The church

  d) All nations

8. Aside from Genesis, where else in Scripture do we find echoes of the Abrahamic promise?

  a) The psalms and the prophets

  b) The Gospels

c) Paul's epistles
d) The book of Revelation
e) All of the above

9. If we are those who inherit not only the privilege of Abrahamic blessing, but also the responsibility of being a blessing to the nations, then what is required of us?

a) Leaving and going
b) Believing and obeying
c) Preaching and saving
d) Both A & B

10. In Christ we inherit Abraham's blessing. What else of Abraham's do we also inherit?

a) Abraham's covenant
b) Abraham's election
c) Abraham's mission
d) Abraham's motto

CHAPTER 5

People Who Walk in God's Way

You Should Know

- "For I have chosen him, so that he will direct his children and his household after him to keep the way of the Lord by doing what is right and just, so that the Lord will bring about for Abraham what he has promised him" (Gen. 18:19).

- The link between church and mission is ethical.

- Three biblical themes of Genesis 18:19: election, ethics, mission

- The community of Abraham: Old Testament Israel, all those who are in Christ

- *Ze'aqah*: the cry of pain, or the cry for help

- *Sedaqah*: righteousness; a state of affairs, something you aim to achieve

- *Mishpat*: legal ordinance or judgment; a set of actions, something you do

Reflection Questions

1. How does Sodom stand in Scripture as a proverbial prototype of human wickedness and of the judgment of God that ultimately falls on evildoers?

2. Explain how God's promise to Abraham is the foundation stone, or mainspring, of all the mission of God's people throughout history.

3. What does the expression "walking in the way of the Lord" mean? Explain using the two possible pictures of the metaphor offered in this session.

Discussion Question

1. Genesis 18:19 is fundamentally a missional declaration, which explains the reason for election and explains the purpose of ethical living. Explain how and why it is enormously rich and significant for both.

Quiz

1. Genesis 18:19 is a remarkable text for understanding the mission of God's people. What great biblical themes does it tie together?
   a) Election, law, and mission
   b) Election, ethics, and mission
   c) Election, ethics, and salvation
   d) Church, ethics, and mission

2. God's universal promise of blessing is nested within the story of one particularly notorious instance of God's historical judgment of an entire city. Which city?
   a) Jericho
   b) Babylon
   c) Sodom
   d) Jerusalem

3. What does the important technical term ze'aqah mean?
   a) Cry for help
   b) Cry for judgment
   c) Cry of pain
   d) All of the above
   e) Both A and C

4. Looking at Genesis 18:19, what distinctiveness of God's people is an

integral part of the role we are called to play in God's mission of bringing blessing to a world that otherwise stands under his judgment?

a) Legal
b) Missional
c) Electoral
d) Ethical

5. What is the foundation stone, or mainspring, of all the mission of God's people throughout history?

a) God's promise to Noah
b) God's promise to Abraham
c) God's promise to David
d) God's promise to the church

6. What two phrases summarize the content of the Abrahamic family curriculum of ethical education?

a) The way of the law; doing righteousness and justice
b) The way of the Lord; doing righteousness and good works
c) The way of the Lord; doing righteousness and justice
d) The way of the salvation; doing righteousness and good works

7. What pair of words stand at the top of the Old Testament's ethical vocabulary, and form part of the content of the Abrahamic family ethical curriculum?

a) Righteousness and justice
b) Righteousness and salvation
c) Salvation and justice
d) Discipleship and salvation

8. *Mišpat* is what needs to be done in a given situation if people and circumstances are to be restored to conformity with *sedeq/sedaqah*. *Mišpat* is a _____. *Sedeq/sedaqah* is a _____.

a) Set of beliefs; state of affairs
b) Set of actions; state of affairs
c) Set of actions; state of beliefs
d) Set of sayings; state of reality

9. Genesis 18:19 shows us the important link in our biblical theology between what two important themes?

   a) Ecclesiology and soteriology
   b) Soteriology and missiology
   c) Ecclesiology and missiology
   d) Ethics and morality

10. What is always linked to the effectiveness of our mission?

   a) Our laws
   b) Our salvation
   c) Our churches
   d) Our ethics
   e) All of the above
   f) None of the above

CHAPTER 6

People Who Are Redeemed for Redemptive Living

You Should Know

- The first language of redemption in the Bible can be found in Exodus 6:6.

- The exodus was not a movement from slavery to freedom, but from slavery to covenant.

- The centrality of every dimension of mission must come from the cross.

- The portrait of God in a biblical theology of redemption is that of divine redeemer.

- Key Old Testament way the New Testament interprets the cross is through the Exodus

- *Go'el*: kinsman-redeemer, family guardian

- Dimensions of Israel's bondage in Egypt: political, economic, social, and spiritual

- Examples of Israel's redemptive-imitation of the exodus: slave release, Year of Jubilee, forgiveness

Reflection Questions

1. The Hebrew word *go'el* is sometimes translated "kinsman-redeemer" or "family guardian." Explain the three examples of how somebody might act as this redeemer in Old Testament Israel.

2. The exodus was not a movement from slavery to freedom, but from slavery to covenant. Explain how this redemption had a clear covenantal and spiritual intent and results.

3. What does it mean to see the exodus in the light of the cross? Why does all Christian mission flow from the cross?

Discussion Question

1. The story of the exodus portrays at least four dimensions of the bondage that Israel suffered in Egypt. Explain and summarize how God redeemed them in every one of these dimensions, and how this relates to the holistic gospel and mission.

Quiz

1. When do we first encounter the language of redemption in the Bible?

   a) Genesis
   b) Exodus
   c) Matthew
   d) Romans

2. The exodus redemption is clearly a major theme for our:

   a) Biblical theology
   b) Systematic theology
   c) Historical theology
   d) Practical theology

3. The Hebrew noun for the person who performs the verb *ga'al* and its action is *go'el*. What does this word mean?

   a) Kinsman-redeemer
   b) Family guardian
   c) Law-giver
   d) All of the above
   e) Both A & B

4. What dimension of the bondage that Israel suffered in Egypt does the exodus show God redeemed them from?

    a) Political
    b) Economic
    c) Social
    d) Spiritual
    e) All of the above

5. When God redeemed his people from an intolerable hell of suffering in Exodus, it led to the inauguration of a society. What was built into their founding documents?

    a) Limitation on government power
    b) Respect for human life and basic rights
    c) Passion for social justice
    d) All of the above

6. What was the motivation for the exodus and God's redemption of Israel?

    a) God's compassionate concern for people suffering under cruel oppression
    b) God's faithfulness to his covenant promises to Abraham
    c) God's desire to pay for their sins and purchase a place for them in heaven
    d) Both A & B

7. What does the New Testament present through the lens of the exodus?

    a) The ethical teachings of Jesus
    b) The redeeming death of Jesus
    c) The victorious resurrection of Jesus
    d) The exalted ascension of Jesus

8. In the Old Testament and New Testament, what act of God is him standing up as the great champion of his people, exerting his mighty strength, and paying the full cost of rescuing them from all that opposes and oppresses?

a) Creation
b) Covenant
c) Redemption
d) Both B & C

9. In both the Old and New Testaments, redemption was considered:

a) A historical fact of the past
b) A personal experience to be enjoyed in the present
c) A status that was to be lived out in ethical response
d) All of the above

10. When we think of the mission of God's people in holistic or integral terms, it is vital that we keep this key biblical concept central to every dimension of mission that we engage in:

a) Creation
b) Covenant
c) Church
d) Cross

CHAPTER 7

People Who Represent God to the World

You Should Know

- "You shall be holy, for I the Lord your God am holy" (Lev. 19:2 ESV).

- Holiness in Leviticus 19 includes: economic justice in employment rights, social compassion to the disabled, sexual integrity, and no ill-treatment of ethnic minorities

- "You are the salt of the earth. But if the salt loses its saltiness, how can it be made salty again? It is no longer good for anything, except to be thrown out and trampled underfoot. You are the light of the world. A town built on a hill cannot be hidden. Neither do people light a lamp and put it under a bowl. Instead they put it on its stand, and it gives light to everyone in the house. In the same way, let your light shine before others, that they may see your good deeds and glorify your Father in heaven" (Matt. 5:13–16).

- Sequence of 1 Peter 2:9–10: "You are a chosen people, a royal priesthood, a holy nation, God's special possession, that you may declare the praises of him who called you out of darkness into his wonderful light. Once you were not a people, but now you are the people of God; once you had not received mercy, but now you have received mercy."

- Sequence of Salvation in the Old Testament: grace, faith, obedience

- The basic principle flowing through biblical theology, ethics, and mission: commands follow grace

- Tasks of priests include: teaching the law of God to the people, bringing the sacrifice of the people to God

- *Qados*: holy, different, distinct

Reflection Questions

1. Grace came first, faith next, and obedience to the law a necessary third, as a believing response in action to what God had already done. Explain the significance of this progression, and what it says about the relationship between law and grace.

2. The mission of God's people includes being God's priesthood in the world. Explain what this means and how this role looks practically in the world.

3. Briefly explain how the bulk of Leviticus 19 shows us that the kind of holiness that reflects God's own holiness is thoroughly practical, social, and very down-to-earth. Why is it true that there is no biblical mission without biblical holiness?

Discussion Question

1. How is the future grace of God's ultimate mission to the nations held alongside the past grace of God's historical act of redemption? And in what way is the whole story of Old Testament Israel and our own missional response to God slung between these two poles of grace and glory?

Quiz

1. According to Exodus 19:3–6, who are we and what are we here for?
    a) We are God's treasured possession and called to obey him
    b) We are a holy nation and called to be a kingdom of priests
    c) We are God's children saved for heaven and its rewards
    d) A & B
    e) All of the above

2. The speech of God in Exodus 19:1–6 is a crucial hinge between what great stories in the first and second halves of the book?

   a) Redemption; violating the covenant, the giving of the law, and the construction of the tabernacle
   b) Redemption; making the covenant, the giving of the law, and the construction of the tabernacle
   c) Redemption; making the covenant, the receiving of the law, and the construction of the temple
   d) Redemption; making the covenant, the giving of the law, and the construction of the palace

3. When God tells Moses to speak to the Israelites the reminder "You yourselves have seen what I did . . .", to what was he pointing?

   a) God's miracles
   b) God's power
   c) God's grace
   d) God's glory

4. By the command of Christ, rooted in the prior reality of God's grace in sending Jesus into the world, we are:

   a) Sent out in mission
   b) Sanctified from our sins
   c) Saved for heaven
   d) Both B & C

5. God had rescued one particular nation out of bondage through the exodus. But what was his ultimate goal?

   a) To offer salvation to all the elect
   b) To offer salvation to all the church
   c) To offer salvation to all the nations
   d) To offer salvation to all the saved

6. When it comes to the mission of God's people, all our missional response to God lies between:

   a) Grace and glory
   b) Historical salvation and ongoing mission
   c) What God has done and what God will yet do

d) Where we have come from and where we are going
e) All of the above

7. Priests stood in the middle, between God on the one hand and all the rest of the people on the other. In that intermediate position, what was their task?

a) Teaching the law of God to the people
b) Ruling over the people and leading them to conquer the nations
c) Bringing the sacrifice of the people to God
d) A and C
e) All of the above

8. What kind of function was the priesthood of the people of God, standing in continuity with their Abrahamic election and impacting the nations?

a) Missional
b) Theological
c) Practical
d) Ethical

9. At heart, what does the Hebrew word for "holy" (*qados*) mean?

a) Perfect
b) Good
c) Different
d) Righteous

10. The strong ethical demand of holiness in Old Testament Israel meant living what kind of lives in every area?

a) Lives of conformity, justice, and compassion
b) Lives of integrity, justice, and perfection
c) Lives of integrity, merit, and compassion
d) Lives of integrity, justice, and compassion

People Who Attract Others to God

You Should Know

- Our greatest motivation for our mission is the name of the Lord Jesus Christ should be known to the ends of the earth.

- God "wears" Israel for the purpose of his renown, praise, and honor.

- The people of all nations are the children of Israel who will return to Zion.

- The Magi are a symbol of the nations bringing their wealth in gratitude to God.

- "You are the light of the world. A town built on a hill cannot be hidden. Neither do people light a lamp and put it under a bowl. Instead they put it on its stand, and it gives light to everyone in the house. In the same way, let your light shine before others, that they may see your good deeds and glorify your Father in heaven" (Matt. 5:14–16).

- Christian women can "win" their husbands through their character and behavior.

- Missional magnetism: God's people are to live in such a way that they become attractors to the God they worship

Reflection Questions

1. Suggesting the mission of God's people is 'cosmetic' is often misunderstood, for the word has come to mean something merely

external and superficial, something just to make you look good. What is the meaning of the original Greek word? How does it relate to the mission of God's people?

2. According to 1 Kings 8:60–61, why is the combination of mission and ethics clear? Why is right living important to mission?

3. Disciples of Christ are to shine with a light that is visible and attractive; this light consists of "good deeds." Explain this concept and offer an example of how it might look.

Discussion Question

1. Isaiah 60 has a strongly missional message in connecting the light of God himself, the light of God's people in the world, and the light that the world will come to live and walk in. Explain and summarize this missional light, particularly how that light impacts both Israel and the nations.

Quiz

1. God's people are to live in such a way that they become:
    a) Attractors to themselves
    b) Attractors to the God they worship
    c) Attractors to the church they worship in
    d) Attractors to the faith they believe in

2. Deuteronomy 4:5–8 puts Israel's obedience on a wide-open stage and invites them to envisage what whom will think as they observe the national life of the people whose God is Yahweh?
    a) The nations
    b) The church
    c) The Israelites
    d) God himself
    e) All of the above

3. What is a vital factor in the attraction of the nations to the living God — even if only at first out of curiosity?

a) The biblical quality of life of God's people
b) The theological quality of life of God's people
c) The ecclesial quality of life of God's people
d) The ethical quality of life of God's people

4. What did Solomon's prayer in 1 Kings 8:41–43 assume?

a) People of other lands will hear of the reputation of Yahweh the God of Israel
b) People from afar will be attracted to come and worship Israel's God for themselves and seek answers to prayer from that God
c) Israel's God can and will hear the prayers of such foreigners and will want to answer them
d) All of the above

5. What should be the greatest motivation for our mission?

a) The conversion of people to the Christian faith
b) The salvation of souls from hell
c) The name of Jesus Christ should be known to the ends of the earth
d) The name of our church would be recognized and respected

6. When it comes to the world knowing who God is and attracting others to want to know him and come pray to him, what combination is clearly crucial?

a) Mission and ethics
b) Theology and mission
c) Evangelism and ethics
d) Mission and evangelism

7. In choosing Israel, God had a wider agenda—namely, the exaltation of his own name among the nations through what he would ultimately accomplish. To what does God compare this covenant with Israel in Jeremiah 13?

a) A piece of equipment
b) A piece of jewelry

c) A piece of clothing
d) None of the above

8. Israel had experienced exile and scattering among the nations, and the prophet Isaiah pictures the nations bringing their children back home. In the wider Old Testament perspective, who will these children of Israel be, returning to Zion?

a) Ethnic Israelites
b) The children of Israel
c) The elect church
d) People of all nations

9. The prophet Isaiah pictured nations from all points of the compass bringing precious wealth in gratitude to God for the salvation that has come to them. Who was it that symbolized this vision as prototypical of the gifts of all nations?

a) The Queen of Sheba
b) The Magi
c) King Solomon
d) King Xerxes

10. Disciples of Christ are to shine with a light that is visible and attractive. What does that light consist of?

a) Right beliefs
b) Good deeds
c) Good theology
d) Right evangelism

CHAPTER 9

People Who Know the One Living God and Savior

You Should Know

- Knowing God is about personal devotion, personal spiritual experience, comprehensive social agenda, and a responsibility that generates a mission.

- "All the things the Lord your God did for you in Egypt before your very eyes" (Deut. 4:34) were part of the Sinai theophany and Exodus deliverance

- "There is no other . . ." is an important feature common to Deuteronomy 4:32–39 and Acts 4:1–22.

- The thrust of the verses in Deuteronomy 4 is filled out in many other Old Testament passages, where we find a combination of the assertion that Yahweh is incomparable and unique.

- "Salvation is found in no one else, for there is no other name under heaven given to mankind by which we must be saved" (Acts 4:12).

- Biblical monotheism: the uniqueness of Yahweh in the Old Testament combined with the uniqueness of Jesus in the New Testament, who are one and the same divine reality

- The *Shema*: "Hear, O Israel: The Lord our God, the Lord is one. Love the Lord your God with all your heart and with all your soul and with all your strength" (Deut. 6:4-5).

Reflection Questions

1. What does it mean that to know God is to be challenged to make God known? In what way does being entrusted with the knowledge of God necessitate that knowledge be shared? Explain.

2. If Moses exhorts Israel about what they must "know" on the foundation of what they have experienced of God's miraculous power, in what way does Peter do exactly the same in Acts 4? And how does he draw his great evangelistic conclusion from this?

3. What is *biblical monotheism*? How does it relate to the mission of God's people?

Discussion Question

1. As in the days of the apostles, there are many today who do not accept that Jesus is the only Savior and Lord and have never even heard of Jesus. And as in the days of Deuteronomy, the people of God live surrounded by multiple cultures that manifest all the idolatries that human beings are capable of. Explain how our days mirror those days, giving clear examples. How does this relate to the mission of God?

Quiz

1. Knowing God has to do with:
   a) Personal devotion and spiritual experience
   b) Communal devotion and comprehensive social agenda
   c) Personal and communal responsibility, generating an agenda of mission
   d) All of the above

2. In Acts 4 and Deuteronomy 4, the speakers in the texts refer to unique events that have been witnessed and that lead to certain conclusions about God–things that are to be:

  a) Known and understood
  b) Known and argued
  c) Known and made known
  d) Known and made believable

3. In Deuteronomy 4, what events does Moses refer to in his claim that nothing like them has ever happened before?

  a) Sinai theophany; exodus deliverance
  b) Sinai legislation; exodus deliverance
  c) Abraham's calling; Sinai theophany
  d) Abraham's calling; Noah's deliverance

4. What the disciples had known about Jesus, what the Israelites had known about Yahweh, had all arisen out of:

  a) Biblical evidence
  b) Personal experience
  c) Historical experience
  d) Theological argument
  e) All of the above

5. Peter and John could speak about "what we have seen and heard" because they were actually present with Jesus. We can't speak in exactly the same way; we depend on:

  a) Their testimony
  b) The Bible
  c) Our personal experience
  d) A & B
  e) B & C

6. What expression is a feature that Deuteronomy 4 and Acts 4 both share?

  a) "You shall love the Lord your God"
  b) "You are witnesses of these things"
  c) "There is no other"
  d) None of the above

7. All that Israel had so uniquely experienced was so that they would learn something utterly vital about:

a) The identity of the living God
b) The laws of the living God
c) The miracles of the living God
d) The blessings of the living God

8. The thrust of the verses in Deuteronomy 4 is filled out in many other Old Testament passages, where we find a combination of the assertion that Yahweh is:

a) Comparable and unique
b) Comparable and rivaled
c) Incomparable and rivaled
d) Incomparable and unique

9. When Peter said in Acts 4, "Salvation is found in no one else, for there is no other name under heaven given to mankind by which we must be saved," who was he speaking about?

a) Elohim
b) Yahweh
c) Jesus
d) None of the above

10. The great truths of Deuteronomy 4, which Israel was to "know and take to heart," are combined in the clinching affirmation and command of:

a) The Ten Commandments
b) The *Shema*
c) The psalms
d) The Holiness Codes

CHAPTER 10

People Who Bear Witness to the Living God

You Should Know

- The Great Commission's focus is disciple-making.

- You had to live under the reign of God if you wanted to go preach about the reign of God.

- We're not all called to be evangelists, but we are all called to be witnesses.

- Two problems standing in the way of God's new-exodus mission are the ignorance of the nations and the blindness of Israel.

- Duties of a witness in Old Testament Israel included: failure to speak up and testify about any matter you had seen or heard was regarded as a sin; primary responsibility must be taken for the execution of the court's verdict; perjury cost the witness their life; the truth of statements or claims were established by witnesses.

- Three key truths are embedded in the great claims that Yahweh makes in Isaiah 43: Yahweh alone is the transcendent, eternal God; Yahweh alone is in sovereign control of history; Yahweh alone is Savior.

- Events of the historical Jesus: the coming Messiah, Jesus's suffering, Jesus's death, Jesus's resurrection

Reflection Questions

1. What is the connection between the words of Jesus to his disciples on both occasions in Luke 24:48 and Acts 1:8 and the words of Yahweh to Israel in Isaiah 43:10, 12 and 44:8? What are the implications of that connection for our witnessing mission?

2. The two great problems that stand in the way of God's great plan are the ignorance of the nations and the blindness of Israel. Briefly summarize and explain these problems.

3. The apostle John provides two "witnesses" as examples of the ongoing testimony to the gospel of Christ: the Samaritan woman and the Holy Spirit. Briefly explain and summarize how they stand as models and encouragement for our own witness.

Discussion Question

1. The New Testament develops the rich Old Testament theme of God's people as Yahweh's witnesses in two ways: the original witness of the historical Jesus and the ongoing testimony to the gospel of Christ. Explain and summarize this double role of witnesses in the New Testament. Offer one way you yourself can witness in these ways.

Quiz

1. It takes disciples to make disciples, and Jesus spent three years teaching his disciples what it meant to be one. In short, you had to live under the reign of God if you wanted to:

    a) Practice the reign of God
    b) Believe the reign of God
    c) Discover the reign of God
    d) Preach about the reign of God

2. Those who know God are required to make God known, which requires the medium of:

a) Words

b) Deeds

c) Evangelism

d) None of the above

e) Both A & B

3. What two terms encompass the verbal dimension of the word-focused mission of God's people?

a) Arguing our case; announcing good news

b) Provoking witness; announcing good news

c) Bearing witness; announcing good news

d) Bearing witness; arguing our case

4. What great problem stands in the way of God's great plan of new exodus?

a) The ignorance of the nations

b) The sin of the nations

c) The blindness of Israel

d) The ignorance of Israel

e) All of the above

f) A and C

5. In Isaiah 43:8–13, who will speak for Yahweh in the great international court of nations and alleged gods?

a) Babylon

b) Israel

c) Rome

d) America

6. Witnessing to the truth about Yahweh as the one true living God is at the heart of the role and mission of a servant—always was and still is. Who is that servant?

a) Israel/Jacob

b) Descendants of Abraham

c) Jewish believers only

d) Both A & B

7. What truth about the living God is to form the substance of the testimony that God's people must bear before the nations?

    a) His identity

    b) His sovereignty

    c) His saving power

    d) All of the above

8. Upon what does all our witness to the Lord Jesus Christ and the saving power of the gospel depend?

    a) The trustworthiness of our testimony

    b) The trustworthiness of our theology

    c) The trustworthiness of the church

    d) The trustworthiness of the Bible

9. Who does the apostle John intend to make a model for a self-replicating evangelistic force for all who come to faith?

    a) Abraham's wife Sarah

    b) Bathsheba

    c) The Samaritan woman

    d) Mary Magdalene

10. Who or what bears witness to Jesus through the witness of his disciples?

    a) The Bible

    b) The Holy Spirit

    c) The church

    d) Theological truth

CHAPTER 11

People Who Proclaim the Gospel of Christ

You Should Know

- The beginning of the biblical Gospel can be found in the book of Genesis.

- Sequence for Isaiah 52:7: "How beautiful on the mountains are the feet of those who bring good news, who proclaim peace, who bring good tidings, who proclaim salvation, who say to Zion, 'Your God reigns'!" (Is. 52:7).

- The beneficiaries of God's redemption are all the nations.

- God's reign begins with Jesus's arrival.

- Paul's missionary goal was ethical transformation.

- The Gospel is the story of Jesus in light of Scripture, a new redeemed humanity, a message to be communicated, ethical transformation, truth to be defended, and the power of God transforming the universe.

- The meaning of the word *gospel*: good news

- *Basar*: Hebrew for "bring or announce good news"

- *Shalom*: peace, wholeness, fullness of life

Reflection Questions

1. When it comes to surveying "*evangel-*" there are two good reasons

for taking a look at the Old Testament. What are those reasons, and why are they good ones?

2. What are all of the spiritual blessings we have received in Christ? Briefly summarize them here.

3. When it comes to the gospel, what truths need to be defended? Why do they need defending?

Discussion Question

1. What are the six ways Paul uses "gospel" in his letters? Briefly explain and summarize these ways.

Quiz

1. The old English word "gospel" means "good news," which is also the core of which "*evangel-*" word in the New Testament?

   a) Evangelism
   b) Evangelists
   c) Evangelical
   d) Evangelistic
   e) Evangelization
   f) All of the above

2. The biblical gospel begins in what book of the Bible?

   a) Genesis
   b) Revelation
   c) Matthew
   d) Acts

3. The messenger's good news of Isaiah 52 consists of three words in verse 7 that could be presented in quotation marks as the words he gasps out as he runs nearer until at last he reaches the city itself and calls out to those within, "Your God reigns!" What are they?

   a) "It's heaven!" "It's good!" "We're saved!"
   b) "It's peace!" "It's judgment!" "We're saved!"

    c) "It's peace!" "It's good!" "We're saved!"

    d) "It's heaven!" "It's judgment!" "We're saved!"

4. When were the prophetic words of Isaiah 61:1–3, which Luke 4:16–19 quotes Jesus reading, fulfilled?

    a) In and through Moses's life and ministry

    b) In and through Jesus's life and ministry

    c) In and through Jesus's second coming

    d) In and through believer's life and ministry

    e) All of the above

    f) B and D

5. What is found among those who understand their mission, to make peace, to do good, and to proclaim God's salvation?

    a) Heaven

    b) The reign of God

    c) The church of Christ

    d) A social gospel

6. The prophets proclaimed God himself would bring the exile to a true end and send a messenger to prepare the way for his return. Who did Jesus identify as the one who fulfilled that role of the Elijah to come pave the way for his arrival?

    a) Matthew the tax collector

    b) John the seer

    c) John the Baptist

    d) Paul the apostle

7. What does the name Jesus mean?

    a) Yahweh is spiritual

    b) Yahweh is heaven

    c) Yahweh is help

    d) Yahweh is salvation

8. What is the "peacemaking" work of the cross that creates one new humanity in relation to the gospel?

    a) A by-product of the gospel

    b) The heart of the gospel

    c) Inconsequential to the gospel

    d) Both A & B

9. "The work of the gospel" seems to refer primarily to what task?

    a) Making the good news believed by all communication possible and whatever cost

    b) Making the good news believed by all deeds possible and whatever cost

    c) Making the good news known by all communication possible and whatever cost

    d) Making the good news plausible by all arguments possible and whatever cost

10. Radical change of life goes along with faith in the good news. They cannot be separated. What kind of transformation does this require?

    a) Ethical transformation

    b) Spiritual transformation

    c) Sinful transformation

    d) Theological transformation

CHAPTER 12

People Who Send and Are Sent

You Should Know

- Evangelism in Romans 10:13–14 includes sending, preaching, hearing, believing, and calling.

- The objective of God's sending his people is to act as agents of his deliverance and declare a message that somebody needs to hear.

- The first description of a person being sent by God is the story of Joseph.

- Moses acted as God's agent of both salvation and revelation.

- Jeremiah was the prophet who indicated the nature of the inspiration of Scripture.

- The perfect missionary is the Word of God.

- The essence of apostleship includes: being sent into the world, commissioning for a task.

- *Salah*: Hebrew word for "to send"

Reflection Questions

1. What is Paul's argument in Romans 10:13–15, and how does it relate to the need for "heralds"?

2. It is God, not the messenger, who is in control of outcomes. That great hope is grounded in two other things that the Old Testament

refers to as being sent by God—God's Spirit and God's Word. What role do they each play in God's message mission?

3. What is the marvelous interlocking network of sending in the New Testament presentation of God's involvement in the mission of Jesus and the church? How does this "interlocking network" show that the sending mission is a participation in the life of God?

Discussion Question

1. The Old Testament segment of our journey of biblical theology on the theme of "sending" has given us three main things to consider: sending for salvation and revelation; sending with authority; sending and suffering. Explain and summarize these themes. How do they relate to the church's current mission as the people of God?

Quiz

1. People must call on Christ for salvation, but to call on him, they must believe in him. And to believe in him, they must:
   a) Understand him
   b) Experience him
   c) Embrace him
   d) Hear him

2. Who is it who sends the authorized "heralds," or messengers, with the good news by which people can be saved?
   a) The church
   b) The pope
   c) Jesus Christ
   d) Paul the apostle

3. When God sends people, what is most often the reason?
   a) To act as agents of his salvation
   b) To declare a message that somebody needs to hear
   c) To act as agents of heaven

  d) All of the above
  e) Both A & B

4. The role of heralds and ambassadors was of great social and political importance. Within this cultural context, who of Israel functioned with Yahweh's authority, claiming to speak for him because they had been sent by him?

  a) The prophets
  b) The poets
  c) The judges
  d) The kings

5. Who was the fulfillment of the promise that God would raise up "a prophet like Moses?"

  a) Isaiah
  b) Amos
  c) John the Baptist
  d) Jesus Christ

6. What is the perfect missionary, bearing fruit entirely as God plans?

  a) God's church
  b) God's people
  c) God's Word
  d) God's creation

7. Ultimately the accomplishment of God's mission does not depend on human agents, but on the sovereign power of God, working through what?

  a) His Spirit
  b) His Word
  c) His church
  d) His creation
  e) Both A & B

8. For what specific missional task did Jesus send the Spirit?

  a) Salvation and revelation
  b) Salvation and judgment

    c) Salvation and spiritual experience

    d) Revelation and spiritual experience

9. What is the essence of apostleship?

    a) Being sent into the world

    b) Commissioning for a task

    c) Defending the faith

    d) Planting new churches

    e) All of the above

    f) A & B

10. Which two areas did John the apostle commend Gaius for his faithfulness?

    a) Faithfulness to the truth; faithfulness to John

    b) Faithfulness to the truth; faithfulness to the brothers and sisters

    c) Faithfulness to the program; faithfulness to the brothers and sisters

    d) Faithfulness to the truth; faithfulness to the program

CHAPTER 13

People Who Live and Work in the Public Square

You Should Know

- According to Genesis 1–2, work is God's idea for our identity.

- As auditor of what happens in the public arena God requires integrity and transparency.

- Our response in the public square in light of God's redemption is constructive engagement and courageous confrontation.

- Our manner of engagement in the public square should be as saints.

- "Blessed are you when people insult you, persecute you and falsely say all kinds of evil against you because of me because of me. Rejoice and be glad, because great is your reward in heaven, for in the same way they persecuted the prophets who were before you" (Matt. 5:11–12).

- The gate: the word used in Old Testament for "public square"

- Cultural mandate: all that we are and do in the public sphere of work, whether at the level of individual jobs, or of the family, or of whole communities, right up to whole cultures and civilizations over historical time, is connected to our createdness and is therefore of interest to our Creator.

Reflection Questions

1. Joseph, Daniel, and Esther all served at top levels in pagan imperial governments and proved that even in such positions they could serve

God and God's people. What do we learn from them about serving in the public square?

2. "Seek the *šalom* of the city to which I have carried you" (Jer. 29:7a). What does this mean and how does it look to seek the *šalom* or welfare of the city?

3. Why is discerning the gods of the public square a crucial, missional task? How are we equipped to resist them?

Discussion Question

1. Briefly summarize and explain the key assertions the Bible makes about the public square. How do each of these assertions contribute to a biblical theology of life?

Quiz

1. According to Genesis 1–2, what is work?
   a) Society's idea for our identity
   b) God's punishment for our sins
   c) God's idea for our identity
   d) Society's punishment for our failures

2. There is a natural creation necessity for trade and exchange between groups living in different places to meet common needs. What do these economic relationships require?
   a) Capitalism
   b) Justice
   c) Winners
   d) Socialism

3. All that we are and do in the public sphere of work, whether at the level of individual jobs, or of the family, or of whole communities, right up to whole cultures and civilizations over historical time, is connected to our createdness and is therefore of interest to our Creator. What is this called?

    a) The capitalist mandate
    b) The democratic mandate
    c) The cultural mandate
    d) The political mandate

4. When it comes to market forces and economic activity, what two principles does the Bible stress to avoid sliding into fatalism or determinism?

    a) Human choice, God's ultimate control
    b) God's choice, God's ultimate control
    c) Human choice, human control
    d) Human choice, market control

5. What part of life will be redeemed and restored to God-glorifying productiveness and human-fulfilling enjoyment?

    a) Personal life
    b) Family life
    c) Public life
    d) Animal life
    e) All of the above

6. In light of God's redemption of the public square, how should we respond?

    a) Constructive engagement
    b) Constructive withdrawal
    c) Courageous confrontation
    d) Courageous acquiescence
    e) A and C

7. What do both the Old and New Testaments command us to do with our government?

    a) Protest it
    b) Pray for it
    c) Petition it
    d) Participate in it
    e) All of the above

8. What is essential to Christian distinctiveness, which in turn is essential to Christian mission in the public arena?

- a) Spiritual conviction
- b) Moral integrity
- c) Theological insight
- d) Biblical knowledge

9. Why are Christians called to be ethically distinct in the public square?

- a) We have a different view of the world
- b) We have a different attitude of the world
- c) We have a different home from the world
- d) We have a different place in the world

10. What is an integral part of the lives of multitudes in the Bible who were faithful to God's calling and their mission, especially in the public square?

- a) Exaltation
- b) Popularity
- c) Blessing
- d) Suffering

CHAPTER 14

People Who Praise and Pray

You Should Know

- The goal of all our mission is to worship and glorify God.

- When we come to the New Testament, the redeeming work of God is linked to the responsibility of bringing praise and glory to God in two key texts from Paul and Peter.

- Psalm 96:1–3:

    "Sing to the LORD a new song;
        sing to the LORD, all the earth.
    Sing to the LORD, praise his name;
        proclaim his salvation day after day.
    Declare his glory among the nations,
        his marvelous deeds among all peoples."

- Witness is closely intertwined with worship.

- Abraham's act for Sodom's good was his prayer of intercession.

- Our most effective weapon on mission is prayer.

- The "other Lord's Prayer": "Send out workers into his harvest field"

- Powers working together for the mission of God: the power of God, the power of the gospel, the power of prayer

Reflection Questions

1. How are worship and witness closely intertwined? In what way is worship the means of mission? Offer an example to illustrate.

2. Read Genesis 18:22–33. How did Abraham intercede on behalf of Sodom? How was this act of intercession joining the mission of God?

3. In what way is prayer spiritual warfare? Why does it matter for the mission of God that it is?

Discussion Question

1. Briefly summarize and explain the five ways in which prayer is missional.

Quiz

1. What is the goal of all our mission?
   a) Worship and glory of God
   b) Evangelism and conversion of people
   c) Defense and protection of the faith
   d) All of the above

2. It is not enough to recognize that worship is the ultimate goal of mission. We also need to see how worship is part of:
   a) The mission of mission
   b) The means of mission
   c) The result of mission
   d) The attitude of mission
   e) None of the above

3. In Ephesians 1 and 1 Peter 2, what is linked to the responsibility of bringing praise and glory to God?
   a) The creative work of God
   b) The character of God
   c) The redeeming work of God
   d) The judgment of God

4. What did Abraham do on behalf of Sodom?
   a) Evangelized it
   b) Prayed for it

c) Taught it

d) Protested against it

5. Solomon and Jeremiah believed that God would answer prayer for the glory of his name and for the *šalam* of whom?

a) Those who pray

b) Those who are prayed for

c) The believer who prays

d) The believer who is prayed for

e) Both A & B

f) Both C & D

6. Prayer is to say, "There is a higher throne." Prayer appeals to a higher authority. In short, what kind of act is prayer?

a) Spiritual

b) Ecclesial

c) Political

d) Economical

7. Some have contended there is the Lord's Prayer and then "the other Lord's Prayer," the only other time in the Gospels when Jesus explicitly tells the disciples what to pray. What is the content of that prayer?

a) "Lead us not into temptation"

b) "Lord, help my unbelief"

c) "Send out workers into his harvest field"

d) "Bless me father, for I have sinned"

8. What three powers did Paul believe worked mysteriously together to accomplish the mission of God?

a) The power of God; the power of the gospel; the power of prayer

b) The power of God; the power of the gospel; the power of evangelism

c) The power of evangelism; the power of the gospel; the power of prayer

d) The power of evangelism; the power of the gospel; the power of apologetics

9. The Bible is a story of war. What is our most effective weapon?

    a) Scripture
    b) Prayer
    c) Evangelism
    d) Theology

10. The role of the church, as a "house of prayer" that has inherited one of the prime functions of the temple, is:

    a) "To keep the community and the world in God"
    b) "To keep God in the community and the world"
    c) "To keep justice in the community and the world"
    d) "To keep the community and the world in spirituality"
    e) Both A & B
    f) Both C & D

CHAPTER 15

The Journey So Far and the Journey Ahead

You Should Know

- For all Christians, ecologically responsible behavior is right and good as part of Christian discipleship to the Lord of the earth.

- The gospel is good news that needs to be heard and to be seen.

- The modern-day scandal of indulgences in the pre-Reformation church is an example of the prosperity gospel.

- Two tasks for serious public arena engagement: prophetic and pastoral

- Paul's sequence of the gospel message in Ephesians and Colossians: creation, church, believers

- Integral mission: understanding that evangelism and social responsibility are integrally related in our proclamation and obedience of the gospel, the two are inseparable

- The mission beyond evangelism is: recognition that evangelism and discipleship are *together* integral and essential parts of our mission as God's people

Reflection Questions

1. How does a biblical theology of creation and our responsibility in it relate to a biblical theology of mission?

2. Why is it that neither evangelism nor social responsibility have

primacy in the life of Christian mission? How does it look for the two to form an "integral mission," as modeled after a wheel?

3. The Great Commission, along with all the practice of the New Testament church, tells us that there is *mission beyond evangelism*. What does this mean, and how does this look for the mission of God's people?

Discussion Question

1. What is the story of God's mission that we have seen through our journey through the Bible? Summarize it here.

Quiz

1. The mission of God's people is carried on in and for _____; it centers on _____ of God; and it lays a demanding privilege on _____.

   a) The world; the law; the church
   b) The church; the law; the elect
   c) The world; the gospel; the church
   d) The world; the gospel; the elect

2. What forms of service are viewed as God's calling on different people, which they can put at his disposal as intentionally missional?

   a) Ecology
   b) Medicine
   c) Education
   d) Pastoring
   e) All of the above

3. In what two ways does the church need to take the task of engaging the public arena more seriously?

   a) The prophetic task; the pastoral task
   b) The protesting task; the pastoral task
   c) The prophetic task; the participating task
   d) The protesting task; the participating task

4. What ministry within local churches is the ministry that really counts as missions?

   a) The ministry of the pastor
   b) The ministry of the people
   c) The ministry of the missionary
   d) The ministry of the committee

5. We tend to separate the individual from the cosmic and corporate dimensions of the gospel, and then we tend to prioritize the first. Yet what is Paul's order of the gospel message in Ephesians and Colossians?

   a) Creation, believers, culture
   b) Believers, church, culture
   c) Creation, church, culture
   d) Creation, church, believers

6. From what have we tended to separate believing the gospel?

   a) Proclaiming the gospel
   b) Living the gospel
   c) Learning the gospel
   d) Defending the gospel
   e) Both B & C

7. Which two aspects of Christian mission, while distinct from one another, are related in our proclamation and obedience of the gospel and form an integral mission?

   a) Evangelism and social responsibility
   b) Discipleship and social responsibility
   c) Evangelism and discipleship
   d) Evangelism and overseas missions

8. What truth of the gospel can counteract the postmodern stance of disbelief in any grand narratives, helping people make sense of life?

   a) Our culture's story
   b) Our personal story
   c) The modern story
   d) The Bible's story

9. What Great Commission practices are *together* integral and essential parts of our mission as God's people?

 a) Evangelism and witnessing
 b) Evangelism and discipling
 c) Evangelism and activating
 d) Evangelism and converting
 e) All of the above

10. The missional challenge is reaching the ends of the earth with the gospel. From a missional perspective, where are the "ends of the earth"?

 a) Your own street
 b) Far across the sea
 c) The whole earth
 d) All of the above

Notes

www.ingramcontent.com/pod-product-compliance
Lightning Source LLC
Chambersburg PA
CBHW010920040426
42445CB00017B/1933

* 9 7 8 0 3 1 0 1 1 1 0 0 9 *